Saint Sofia of Pontus
Orthodox Saint
✝ 6 May 1974

Monaxi Agapi
St George Monastery

Published by: Virgin Mary of Australia and Oceania 2020 ©

oceanitissa@gmail.com
www.oceanitissa.com.au
Youtube: Oceanitissa

Cover image created by Anna Skoubourdis. ©

Subscribe to receive updates and Orthodox Christian creative media

www.oceanitissa.com

The monastery of Panagia (Virgin Mary) Kleisoura

The monastery of Panagia Kleisoura can be found between the villages of Varyko and Kleisoura, at the east foothills of mount Mouriki and celebrates on September the 8th. Ecclesiastically, it falls under the administration of the Holy Metropolis of Kastoria.

The monastery was built in its current form at the end of the 17th or the beginning of the 18th century. Its builder, the holy monk Isaias Pistas, a monk at the Holy monastery of Ivires in Mount Athos was originally from Kleisoura and built upon older foundations of the 14th or the 15th century. The building of the catholico –meaning the central church inside the monastery- dedicated to the Birth of Panagia has received numerous alterations, like the widening of its dome in 1911. In the south wing of the monastery there's a chapel dedicated to Saints Constantine and Helen.

The big icon depicting the Birth of Panagia is considered especially miraculous in the monastery. Additionally, another image of Panagia holding the Divine Infant at a unique praying spot with many vigil oil lamps as well as dedications from the faithful is considered miraculous; this icon can be found at the north edge of the magnificent wood carved iconostasis.

At the north-west part of the monastery we find a church with a cemetery dedicated to the memory of the beheaded Saint John the Baptist, with miraculous holy water. To the east, inside the woods, above the monastery we find the seat of the Holy Trinity which must have functioned as a place of solitude of an unknown ascetic – maybe the same holy one who had built the monastery as it happened in most of the cases-

Today, of the sisterhood inside the cloister, the third in order abbess is in charge. After Abbess Dorothea Kornofoliotissa and bbess Anysia, Abbess Efraimia is currently in charge of the monastery. The sisterhood consists of five nuns and one in training (this information is as of 2013).

If Saint Sofia visited the monastery today, she would have found nothing that would remind her of her days there. The nuns, tirelessly like working bees, under the motherly protection of the abbess combined with their own zeal, as well as with the blessings of the local bishop and the spiritual guidance of their spiritual father, have turned the once withdrawn monastery into a workshop of goodness and perfection.

The ancestry of Sofia

The information we have about Sophia we've gathered mainly from people who have met her during her life, her very few relatives, and finally from people that have visited at the time, the monastery. When we started our research in 1989-90, unfortunately there was nothing specific written for this modern hermit. The very few and scattered news we found, we managed to draw from local newspapers or magazines at the time. After 1971, to the north side of the monastery a highway was built so access to the monastery became very easy. Until then, people would climb on foot from the surrounding villages -usually for 4 hours- in order to kneel before the icon of The Virgin and take advice from Sofia the hermit.

Sophia was born in one of the villages over the Adras province at the Metropolis of Trapezounta of Pontus. Daughter of Amanatios Saoulidis and Maria, she was running inside churches and chapels from very young. She was beautiful with brown eyes and a long face. Her hair was blond and she would make them into 5 long braids. Perhaps this was the reason why later on she wouldn't care for it at all. At a very old age for those times, she got married by her parents who were pressured by their relatives. Her parents were God fearing and didn't pressure her; instead they let her decide freely on her own. "In the old country she didn't want to marry. She wanted to be a nun, but her parents married her" (testimony from E.S. from Argyroupoli of Pontus).

During her short marriage with Iordanis Chotokouridis, they had one or two children; but they were devoured by domesticated pigs due to neglect. The husband later disappeared in the work camps in the depths of Pontus. These incidents did not make Sofia desperate, they led her instead into a deep penance and to her ascetic devotion.

So, from Pontus, her country, Sofia started her ascetic life, away from her relatives and alone in the mountain. During a previous prosecution from Turkish militia, Saint George appeared to her on his horse, and after he revealed to her the imminent danger, he ordered her to let the villagers also know to hide. Thus, the village was saved.

About her journey to the motherland Greece as a refugee in 1919, this story is mentioned: The ship she was travelling on was caught in the middle of fierce sea turbulence, and the danger of going down was imminent. They were finally saved. The captain after doing the sign of the cross said: 'You had someone among you and they saved you'. Everybody then looked at Sophia who, isolated in a corner of the ship didn't stop praying during this whole difficult journey. This specific story also exists as an audio recording of her narrating the incident in her own words. She says:

- The waves were filled with angels and then Panagia appeared. The world will be lost she says because you are all sinners.

- Mother of God, dispose of me because I am the sinner, to save the world, Sofia said. The name of the boat was Saint Nicholas.

When they finally reached the Greek shores at the port of Piraeus, the Virgin appeared again and told Sofia:

-You must come to My house. Sofia asked:

-Who are You and where is Your house?

- I am at Kleisoura the Virgin responded.

During the first years of her life, in the monastery at Kleisoura, a male monastery at the time, Father Grigorios Magdalis was in charge. The holy monk was an old resident of Mount Athos; a man of great virtue. Close to him, Sofia was initiated to the spiritual life, and later she always mentioned his name with particular respect.

At the slab of the fireplace

The slab of the fireplace used also as an oven in the main dining hall of the monastery, became the permanent residence of Sofia, by order of The Virgin. She spent all her nights kneeling with her back against the wet wall; she would barely sleep for a couple of hours. There was no window or glass at the time, so the cold and the moisture coming from the running waters, made it even more profound and stinging. The big thermometer outside the gates of the monastery would many times show temperatures below -15 Celsius in the winter. Occasionally, a small fire would manage to survive in the fireplace, but everything was open and the fire would die easily. On the ledge of the window across the mural of The Virgin, a clean candle would be always lit. There she sat, there she ate, as well as spent her time watching the gates of the monastery. Often, without any warning, as there were no telephones or other means of communication, she would mention the pilgrims who would appear shortly after by name, before the others would even take notice of them. And when she wanted to say something, she would stand up from the fireplace and she would suddenly appear in front of them and would speak.

One time, a bus came from the village of Krokos, in Kozani. Sofia greeted everyone by name, and at the same time she mentioned to each one of the visitors their personal or family problems, asking also about those who stayed back at the village. Students of Father Leonidas Paraskevopoulos, who later became a bishop, would come by bus from Thessaloniki to listen and take advice from her. "You have a great treasure up there" the Father used to say. Devout Christians from the outskirts of Thessaloniki, like Stavroupolis and Krya Vrysi, would also visit; even from as far as Athens, people would travel to meet her.

Garments and behavior

Her clothes were very poor. No undergarments. Sometimes during the winter time, she would throw on her shoulder a blanket full of holes, or a shawl eaten by rats. One time in the middle of the winter, some pilgrims who were spending the night at the monastery saw Sofia with a thin dress standing by a brook, possibly created from the pouring rain, cooling down, "throwing water on her neck, to her feet, like someone who wants to cool down from the heat". As she was wearing black clothes, the place had a strange glow which the pilgrims could clearly see. "Grandmother Sofia, weren't you cold at dawn when you were throwing water on you at the brook?" Out of humility she replied: "This is how it seems to you". Then she added: "I am burning for my Christ my dear. This is how you should also be".

Other times she would gather leaves and branches from the trees and place them by the fireplace; then she would curl inside them like a mouse. Sometimes they would catch fire though and she would barely manage to wake up and avoid being burnt alive. At those times, she would wear those burnt old clothes for days, until new ones were found. The pilgrims would see her wearing those clothes in the cold and humidity and would bring her new and clean ones. But she would take them with one hand, and with the other she would give them to the poor. She never had a new garment or a second change. Only when she didn't want to see the people who were bringing her clothes saddened, she would wear them until they left; then she would take them off. She always walked barefoot. She would rarely wear a pair of thick, old, short socks made of wool and full of holes; she would also wear a pair of old slippers or old shoes. "All Saints walked barefoot. Why should I wear shoes?" She was always wearing a black headscarf. Her hair were never washed or combed since she left Pontus, and they turned as hard as the hair of a horse's tail. A pilgrim once told her "Sofia, this head of yours has become like a sheep, why don't you comb your hair?" "I wish I was a sheep" she replied, "I wouldn't want to be anything else". Her head though smelled like a sweet fragrance. She once tried to thin the hair that fell in front of her eyes but she needed to use the scissors the monastery kept to cut sheep wool. Instead of any other smell, even human, her hair had a fragrant smell.

At night, sitting by the fireplace, she would usually ask of anyone able to read, to recite to her the lives of the Saints, from little pamphlets she would keep in her belongings. When the cold was harsh and the visitors would observe her barefoot, they would beg her to let them throw wood in the fireplace. She would shout a long lasting "Noooo", which they can still hear and repeat, in tears.

She arrived at the monastery at the age of 44. To avoid provoking the monks with her beauty, she would smudge and blacken her beautiful face using smoke and dirt from the cauldrons. She would hold the burning coils in her bare hands without fire tongs.

She was always fasting. Red peppers or a leak baked on the fire from the fireplace, some pickled green tomatoes, usually moldy, and when the day permitted it, some salted fish. The weeds, mushrooms, and moss, she would eat raw with lots of salt on top. On Saturday and Sunday, she would use a spoon of olive oil on her meal, whatever that meal was. At other times she would open a can of fish and would eat it days later, after mold would form as thick as a finger. She would place food inside copper-made utensils and would eat them after they turned green from rust; death could be instant for her. She would boil leaves from the trees, and furn. She wouldn't clean the grapes from the ants; neither would she throw away the rotten ones. Despite of all of these practices, no harm came to her. She was always content, and with a deep doxological pleasure she would say: "My heart rejoiced".

She would never cook for herself. But, when they expected visitors, she would make the women prepare beans or barley; sometimes with oil and sometimes without, yet, it always came out enough for all to eat no matter how much they put in the pan. Nobody was ever left hungry. "Are you hungry?" she would ask. "Come, let me give you food". She would prepare coffee for the pilgrims, as well as for those just passing by. She never washed the coffee pot; it was almost full from coffee sediments. No one was allowed to wash it. But nobody seemed to bother, no matter how dirty it looked.

People would mostly find her bent as always, sweeping the Virgin's yard. All were welcome and accepted. "Welcome, welcome, come my children, sit. Are you from Pontus my children? Welcome, welcome. You must have faith. Virgin Mary weeps for you. Have strong faith. Keep fasting. You are out there in this world. You reap what you sow. Perform charity. Help those in need. Keep fasting and be vigil. Never abandon prayer. Praying saves people". And when the time came for them to leave, she would walk them off doing the sign of the cross, until they would disappear in the horizon.

She never hurt or upset a human being. When she realized people were struggling because of the sins that tortured them, she would pass by them discretely. She would whisper a couple of words like a password, without the rest of the group being able to listen or realize what she was saying, and she would distance herself again. The person would then understand and follow her. They would both sit alone away from the rest so that they wouldn't be seen or heard by the rest. Without asking for the sin or the problem, she would first comfort them and then offer advice with kind and good for the soul words of God. Other times, she would say "They came black in front of The Virgin and they leave white".

She especially cared about single girls who happened to stray away from the right path. She would gather them around her and advised them better than a mother would. She asked them not to speak again of their fall and made sure they had good marriages, giving them even a dowry from the offerings people made to her. "The Holy Mother will not leave you" she used to say.

She lived in misery and poverty. When the conditions were becoming extremely rough, down at the fireplace, she would go to the upper floor in cell number one. She would use leaves and straws as a mattress, and lie on top of them. The curiosity of people made them search even under the leaves and what did they find? Sharp, pointy rocks placed under the straws. During the German occupation of the Second World War, she would hide oil and other provisions which she later distributed to those in great need. When rebels were searching to capture her, she would hide under the wild rose bushes. Her behavior was easily misinterpreted. The children coming from the city of Kastoria when they were watching her hiding would say "Come see what Sofia is doing".

She saw a lot of money passing through her hands. She would take them and keep them wherever was most convenient. In bushes, under rocks, inside holes and walls, under the wooden stairs, under the roof tiles. When she needed some she would go find them and offer them to those in need. She witnessed a lot of scandals by people monks and priests, but never accused any of them.

"You see? I don't see. You hear? I don't hear. You know? I don't know".

"Cover yourselves, let God cover you" she used to say.

Students and religious young people, simple people and generals, nuns and abbesses, low clergy and high ranking clergy, even people from Jerusalem and France visited, to witness this emaciated body, to listen to the Word of God. Some would even keep notes of her words, while some foolish people from the near village called her insane, stupid, or stupid-Sofia. She could understand them all, but she wouldn't reply. "Key to the mouth" she used to say, and she kept her word. Always offering a kind word to people, always with a serious and profound gaze. Her looks scared many. "She had long nails, her hands were black. I was scared. I was young and I felt fear. I would see her in my nightmares later".

Her favorite saying was "Be very patient, much patience". She used to repeat it over and over again, she, who her life was only patience and a rough struggle in the name of Christ. Much patience.

Her body resembled that of Saint Mary of Egypt; skeletal and dry, «bony, bones with skin". A face of bones only, with extruded cheek bones. Her eyes were as if she had hollow eye sockets. Her hands were gnarled, burned from the ashes and the coils. Dry skin, sunburnt, yellow, –almost white- as if without blood. Her hair was rough, usually full of holly oak leaves, thorns, and grass.

At one time, Sofia became very ill. She would bend in half from the pain. Her abdomen opened from the illness. Maybe it was appendicitis, maybe a hernia, or a severe respiratory problem. The wound opened and she would try to patch it with pieces of cloth and wicks from the oil lamps. The wound started to rot. It smelled, but she rejected any help or treatment. "The Virgin Mary will come and take the pain away, she promised" she was saying.

She narrates this event to devout pilgrims who came by bus from Athens. This wonderful narration is saved on audio file.

- The Virgin Mary came with Archangel Gabriel and Saint George; other Saints were there also.

The Archangel said: -We shall cut you, now.

I said: - I am a sinner, let me confess, receive Holy Communion and then cut me.

- You shall not die –the Archangel replied-, we will perform surgery on you; and then the Archangel cut me.

She would narrate these events innocently and simplistic, as if it was the most natural thing in the world. And she would lift without any shame her blouse or her dress to show the incision that closed by itself. There was absolutely no doubt in the words coming out of Sofia.

She never paid attention to her illnesses or her wounds. At some point, builders were replacing the roof tiles at the west wing of the monastery. Sofia stepped on a big nail. Not a single sound was heard. No voice, no crying. Yet, this pain is unbearable. The nail had pierced her foot and came across the other side without any blood running. The workers were scared, but she helped them hit it with a lath hammer from the top side to remove it; then she carried on as if nothing had happened.

5. Memories and testimonials

The bishop of the Metropolis of Langadas, Spyridon, originally from Kleisoura remembers the stories told by his parents about Sofia.

"Just like the ill woman in the Gospel, and just like Anna, the daughter of Phanouil, seven years after been a virgin (Luke 2:36-38), Sofia remained at the courtyard of The Virgin and was telling in a simple and undoubtedly convincing manner all the wonders of God and Virgin Mary, over there at the monastery of Kleisoura. I hadn't met her in person because we had left the village before her time, but the stories told by my parents, my godmother, as well as those of other residents in the area, created the image of a venerable, blessed, humble, and charming person".

The now departed Efthimia Saoulidou, wife of her first-born nephew, the late Isaac, treated Sofia with great respect ever since the early years they were travelling with Father Grigorios the abbot to the monastery and back to their house, in Anarrahi. They would leave the horse in the stable and they would take good care of them.

Everybody respected her. How can I say this, she would understand our thoughts and advised Isaac and I towards good. I rented the house to the teachers of the village and they would go visit her, and asked for her enlightened advice. They were teachers, and they would listen to an illiterate woman; that is how enlightened Sofia was. She used to tell me: Let them sleep first, and then shall we. She, as a woman didn't smell, rather, I can say she had a pleasant smell, as

Father Fotios says. He was confessing to her, and she to him.

She would bless the women who didn't have children by doing the sign of the cross using a small icon depicting the birth of the Virgin; she used it to conceal her own prayer and the grace she received from the Mother of the Lord. She would bless other illnesses by doing the sign of the cross using a small icon depicting the Holy Unmercenaries.

Others had witnessed three snakes sleeping next to her at her pillow; they wouldn't hurt her, and she wouldn't hurt them. Once, people escorted her to light the vigil lights in the chapel of the Holy Trinity, when they saw a big snake. They got upset and tried to kill it, when Sofia scolded them. "If it doesn't hurt you, don't hurt it", she added. "It belongs to the church".

In other occasions though, she would chase the snakes and smash their heads with rocks.

The late general Christos Fatousis who used to visit her since his commission in the area during the war and later until 1949, he used to tell an unbelievable story, for today's standards, up until the day he passed away. "Sofia had a bear and was letting her feed from her own palm, bread and anything else. And the big, but harmless animal would take the food, lick her hands and feet out of gratitude, and then would disappear in the woods. She had even given the bear a name; Come my Red, come to eat bread, she would say.

But, for someone who didn't know this happened, to witness it, they would freeze from fear. In the wild mountain at the time, many bears, wolves and other wild animals were wondering around."

Many others witnessed this: the birds would come and sit on her head and she would tell them: "Are you hungry my little birds? Come, I'll give you food". The blessed woman would then put breadcrumbs on the window ledges for the birds and they would gather around her, flying and chirping. When she passed away, the birds would go and pinch a photo of her from the monastery. How many such incidents are written in the scripts found in the monastery.

One day, Sofia was working in the garden. A woman who was glowing approached her and pointed at the crops and told her: Water them my daughter so that the people can eat. Sofia, without realizing who she was, invited this woman to enter the church of The Virgin to worship her. Indeed, she entered and after a while Sofia also stepped in to greet her from up close. But the woman was nowhere to be found. When she later discussed the incident with Father Grigorios, he assured her that the woman she saw was the Virgin.

Sofia lived the following miraculous incident, brought to our attention by a third party. "One day, Sofia said to the Virgin in tears: My Holy Virgin I have no candles, my lamp is broken, I have no matches, I can't come to light your vigil lamps, what am I going to do? The Virgin then appeared to her and told her: Don't be sad, Sofia I will enlighten the people and they will bring you everything you need. At nightfall a woman also called Sofia told her husband Nikolaos, tomorrow I will visit the monastery of the Virgin. This lantern is of no use to us, we don't make tobacco anymore, so I'll take it to Sofia. So, this blessed woman packed candles, matches, as well as a few food provisions (she loved red peppers fried and freshly made and baked bread). As soon as the bus reached the monastery we heard the bells ringing joyfully, and she came to us, glowing. She then said: The Virgin was in the bus with you and she was blessing you. Then she took us all to her hermitage. When my mother's time came, she opened her arms and said to her: The Virgin told me: Come Sofia my child. I enlightened the people and they will bring you whatever you need, come, sit with me near these bags, do you see her? They said we shall go to Sofia and bring her clothes. The only one who didn't brag was the one who brought that bag. She will wear these clothes and as soon as she leaves you, she will remove them. I just want her to see me to be pleased.

Sofia's daughter, Despoina was considering becoming a nun when she was young. And one day, when she was visiting Grandmother Sofia, she told her:

What you are considering is not going to

happen. That is very difficult. When Despoina grew up, she had a family.

At the hermitage of the Holy Trinity located about 300 meters to the east and above the monastery, but a very steep zigzag climb, Sofia climbed day and night to light the vigil light inside the chapel. When people asked her how could she, an old woman, manage to climb so fast, she would respond "the Virgin lifts me up". Yet, some say that they could see her often ascending and descending the mountain without touching the ground; she was flying.

At the same place (the hermitage) the following incident is reported: Mr. Nikos after finishing his night shift visited the monastery with some friends. As soon as they arrived and it was his time to enter, Grandmother Sofia loved him very much, she told him: "My child Nikos, are you here? Will you go to the Holy Trinity; someone just went there and took some money. Will you go catch him and bring him here?" Nikos was very tired, I didn't realize how I managed to climb the mountain, he told us later, and indeed I saw someone descending it. I went near him and asked him "Brother, did you take the money from the chapel?" He nodded, yes. "We must go together to Sofia, she is waiting for us". As soon as we entered the room she told him: "You will never do what you did ever again. It is a great sin. Now, you will return half of the money, and my son Nikos, you will put in the other half".

She was a good friend of the Saints. Saint

George had her under his protection from the time she was living in Pontus, when he saved her village from an attack by paramilitary Turkish troops. The saint was also present during her operation we mentioned before. In the end, Sofia left this world the day we celebrate his memory according to the old calendar.

Saint Minas, the protector of the city of Kastoria, whose icon was present inside the main church of the monastery, many times he appeared as a horseman, and was also heard by other people who used to work there at the time. But Sofia couldn't just hear him; she could also see him clearly surrounded by a bright fog.

About the old calendar, Sofia asked the Virgin and she replied, Sofia, you have two eyes, follow your new one.

So, she never fended off from the Virgin; neither from the monastery, nor from Her church. "We have one glass, one spoon", she used to say. She loved all, and didn't exclude anyone.

Sofia becomes a nun

One of the most regular visitors, almost a student, of Sofia, was the later monk Kyprianos (1935-2013). During his military service at the city of Ptolemaida, soldier Dimitris wanted to be surrounded by spiritual individuals. He was also the spiritual child of the late Elder Philotheos Zervakos, who also served as a prior of the Holy Monastery of

Loggovarda. This is how he connected with Sofia and listened to her spiritual words. Later, as a monk, he was registered at the monastery of Saint Paul in Mount Athos, and founded the monastery of Saint Kyprianos at the city of Oropos. He was the one who first mentioned the holy Abbess Maria Myrtidiotissa to her, and she expressed the wish to go kneel and pray at Kleisoura in order to meet that person of God. It was this acquaintance and friendship that allowed Sofia to become a nun. So, on the 25th of October 1971 (noon), in the main church of the monastery of Kleisoura, Sofia received the tonsure and received the name of Myrtidiotissa. At the time, Maria the Abbess was serving as Abbess of the Holy Monastery of the Annunciation at the town of Oinousses, which belonged ecclesiastically to the Holy Metropolis of the island of Chios; the holy monk Kyprianos belonged to the Holy monastery of Saint Paul, and later to the Holy Monastery of Xenofon in Mount Athos. The only irregularity in this process was the fact that the monastery of Kleisoura was a male monastery. The Abbot serving at the time, holy Monk Nektarios, former resident of the monastery of Ivires at Mount Athos, although present at the monastery did not attend the tonsuring. Three years later, just before her departure from this world, Sofia herself told him: "My child, Nektarios, Kyprianos with the Mother came and made me a nun and called me Myrtidiotissa".

Sofia's long braid, unwashed and filled with waste hair, is kept safe at the Holy Monastery of the Annunciation, at the town of Oinousses. Part of it, is also kept at the Holy Monastery of Prodromos, at the city of Veroia.

Her end

Before her passing Sofia used to say:

-I shall be gone, but soon a great tragedy will fall upon our country.

When Turkey invaded the island of Cyprus on the 20th of July 1974, her students understood her prophesy.

At her funeral, among others, the Abbot of the monastery was present, Archimandrite Nektarios Stergiou. By his request, the eulogy was delivered by Father Chrysostomos Avagiannos, current bishop of Eleftheroupolis, starting with the verse "received the cross … and by doing you taught, looked beyond the flesh. … the care and responsibility of the soul which is something immortal", from the Apolytikion of the Holy women. He was there by his own volition, as was Father Grigorios Chatzinikolaou, both deacons at the Metropolis of Florina. Nobody informed them but the learnt from a divine sign. On behalf of the people of the area as well as the local club, the young teacher George Galitsas talked.

The local club also hosted the forty-day memorial, as well as the yearly memorial of Sofia, with the assistance of her nephew Isaac Saoulidis.

Eight years later, in 1982, her body was exhumed; when they opened the tomb the smell of basil came out, and that intense smell stayed there for many days. Others reported a light coming from the grave and ascending to the sky. A woman suffering from cancer entered her tomb after her exhumation and was cured.

Her graceful remains, after been hidden in various places were finally found inside her grave. Today, the place is transformed into a beautiful monument and her relics are kept with devotion inside the monastery. Many have kept a piece of the rags she used to wear and hold them as precious treasures. Some have small pieces of her relics. The head scarf she was wearing is kept by a devoted pupil of hers in the city of Ptolemaida and performs miracles, mainly for childless and pregnant women alike.